Three's A Crowd

These trios can be performed with any other combination of instruments within the Christmas series.

Christmas

Flute

A mix and match collection of 21 trio arrangements by James Power.

EXCLUSIVELY DISTRIBUTED BY

HAL•LEONARD®

Exclusive distributors:
Chester Music
14-15 Berners Street, London W1T 3LJ, UK.

Music Sales Pty Limited
20 Resolution Drive, Caringbah, NSW 2229, Australia.

Order No. PM2417161R
ISBN 0-7119-9382-3
This book © Copyright 2002 Chester Music.

Instruments featured on the cover provided by Macari's Musical Instruments, London.
Models provided by Truly Scrumptious and Norrie Carr.
Photography by George Taylor.
Cover design by Chloë Alexander.
Printed in the United Kingdom.

Contents

Deck The Hall

Traditional

4

O Come All Ye Faithful

Traditional

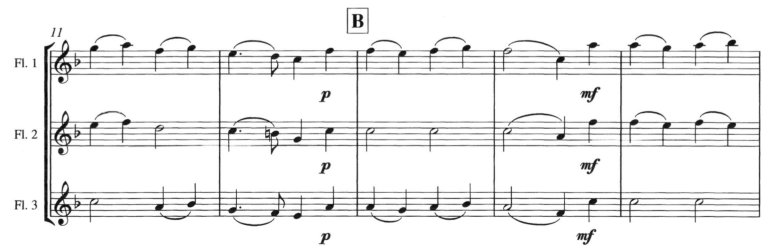

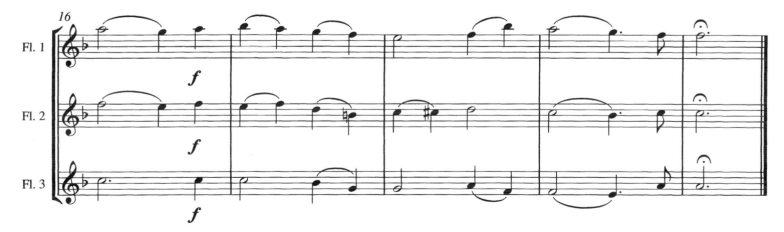

Whilst Shepherds Watched

Music by Tchaikovsky

God Rest Ye Merry, Gentlemen

Traditional

Hark! The Herald Angels Sing

Traditional

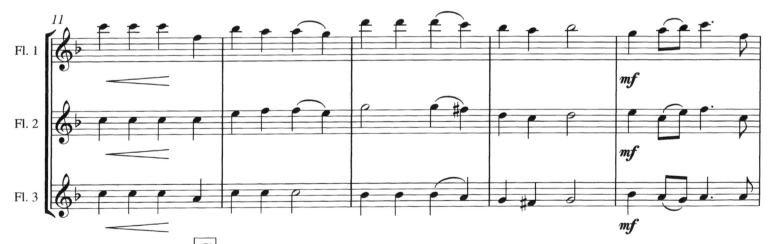

O Little Town Of Bethlehem

Traditional

It Came Upon The Midnight Clear

Traditional

10

The First Nowell

Traditional

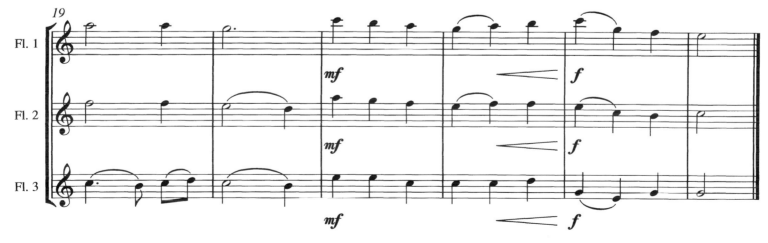

11

Christmas Christmas

Music by James Power

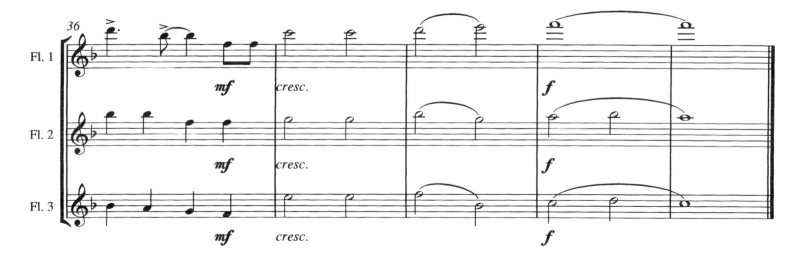

13

Ding Dong! Merrily On High

Traditional

D.S. al Fine

Fine

We Wish You A Merry Christmas

Traditional

Joy To The World

Traditional

Merrily

17

Silent Night

Traditional

Away In A Manger

Traditional

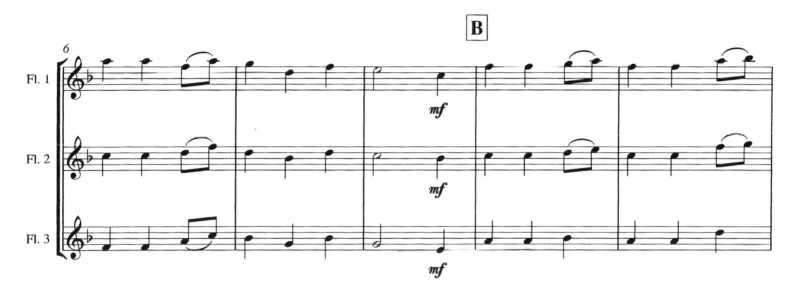

19

Good King Wenceslas

Traditional

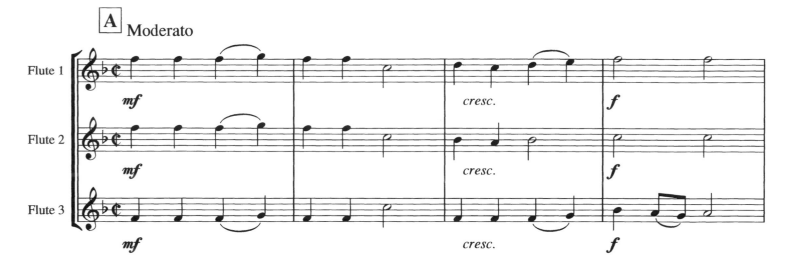

20

Once In Royal David's City

Traditional

We Three Kings

Traditional

A Allegretto

B

C

22

Jingle Bells

Words & Music by J.S. Pierpont

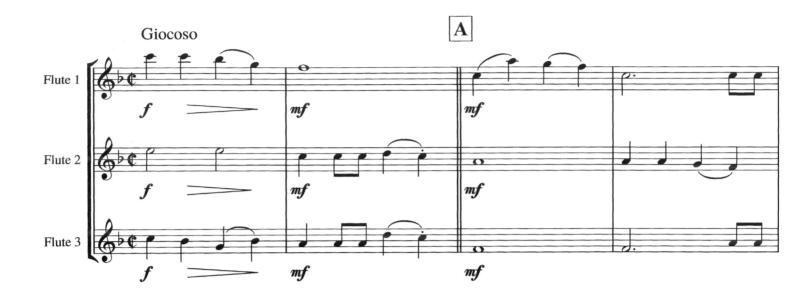

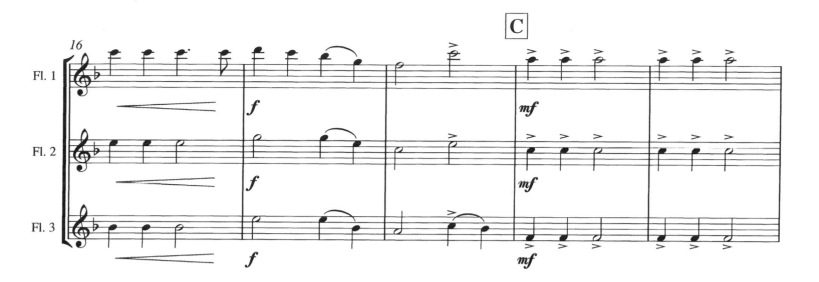

Angels, From The Realms Of Glory

Traditional

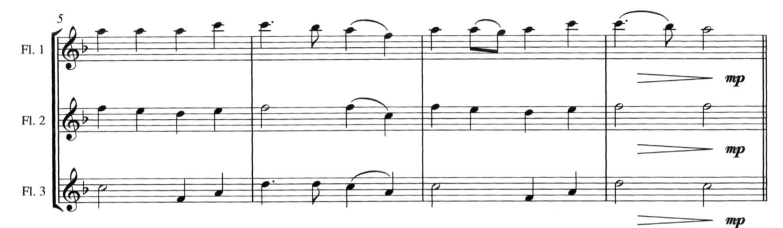

The Holly And The Ivy

Traditional

The Coventry Carol

Traditional

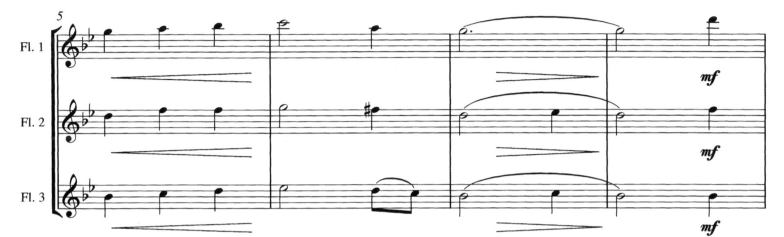

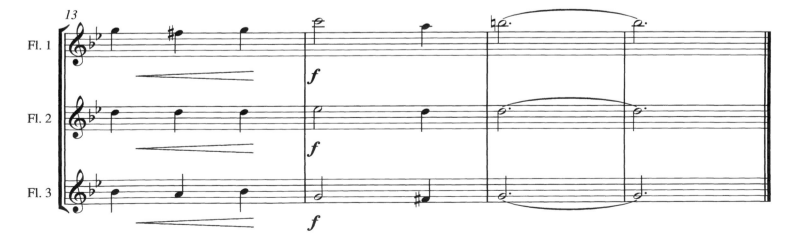

6/09 (169947)